C.H.I.P.S.

(Chameleon's Hiding in Plain Sight)

Developing Todays Sons for Tomorrow's Daughters

TOMMY E. LEWIS, III

Book Cover design by Lindsay Heider Diamond

For information contact Authors Inside
P.O. Box 293, Oceano, CA 93475
Email: **info@authorsinside.org**
Website: www.authorsinside.com

ISBN: 978-1-954736-04-7

First Edition: September 2020

C•H•I•P•S

(Chameleon's Hiding In Plain Sight)

Developing today's Sons for tomorrows Daughters

For my daughter,

BreAnna Faith Tucker,

the most beautiful human soul my heart has ever known.

CONTENTS

The Cycle of Emotional Violence-

EMOTIONAL IMMATURITY EMOTIONAL TURMOIL EMOTIONAL DRIVER EMOTIONAL BLACKMAIL

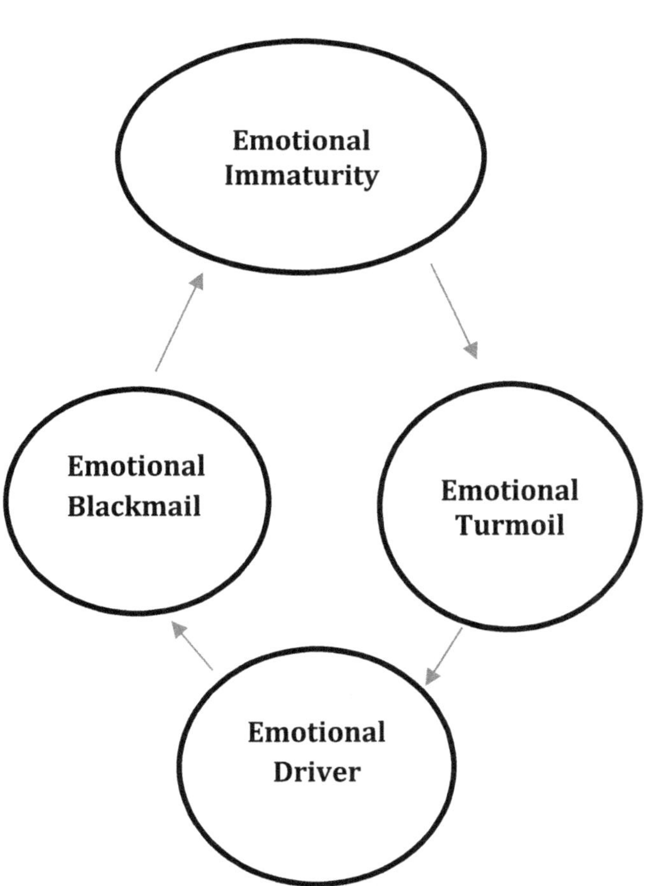

Emotional Immaturity
Highlights a lack of grown, maturity, or sense of responsibility which are characteristics of an adult. Emotions are a powerful force that can drive, hinder, inspire, or motivate you. Whatever the impetus, emotions will drive you in one way or another becoming the fuel of behavior and motivation for any particular direction.

Emotional Turmoil
I know that what I am doing is wrong, yet I do it anyway. I want to be a good person and do the right thing, but it does not always translate into the right action. So I battle within myself. Things happen within me that cause me to feel something and as a result of that feeling I have a wrong reaction and as a result of my internal struggle my woman ends up getting hurt, mistreated, and/or abused.

Emotional Driver
I am caused to feel a sense of discomfort based upon an external circumstance or situation. I feel pain, fatigue, frustration, fear, shame, or any other triggering emotion and I use this as a reason/excuse to compulse.

Emotional Blackmail
Abusive tool used to handcuff her to an unwanted position, but also to cool things off and hide in her emotion as the loving, kind, giving, nurturing "man," until the little boy within surfaces; immature, underdeveloped, unsure, unsteady, and losing the war within, triggered by an event that causes an emotional rush and unable to make the right choices. Repeating the loop until, eventually, the relationship is severed because the pain is unbearable or she is left an empty shell of a human being with an eroding self-worth, trudging along in a "relationship," unhappy and unfulfilled.

CHAPTER ONE

The Cycle of Emotional Violence

Emotional Immaturity

Incorrect teaching when it comes to self-regulation of emotion quickly spirals into infantile/childish reactions vs. mature/adult responses that guide negative emotionality into positive forms of expression.

Expressed or suppressed anger i.e. expressed in disproportionate ways or suppressed into cynicism, resentments, or disdain/contempt towards others is the wrong way to deal with your emotion. Emotional unintelligence and immaturity will keep young boys reacting to emotions i.e. impulsivity, short sighted thinking.

Emotional intelligence and maturity trains men to respond to their emotions positively by self-regulating, weighing options, thinking before acting/speaking, and correctly processing information using spiritual principles, logic, reason, properly harnessed emotion, context, as well as circumstance, so that the end result is positive and healthy vs. negative and unhealthy.

Emotional immaturity always gives you the quickest and easiest "solutions." Emotional immaturity fosters and reinforces gender stereotypes and inequality in relationships and breeds dysfunction, unrealistic expectations, and co-dependence.

- In what ways has Emotional Immaturity blinded you from your responsibility when inappropriately dealing with a situation or aided in the demise of platonic or romantic relationships?

Emotional Turmoil

Emotional Turmoil is an internal roller coaster that keeps an emotionally immature male fighting within himself, fluctuating from one extreme feeling to another. When a man is feeling loving then the level of kindness, consideration, compassion, understanding, and care is at its apex. If triggered into a negative feeling of emotion then the level of mean-spiritedness, rudeness, callousness, disregard, and selfishness goes to its extremes. In each instance, it's a lack of control that pushes the emotion in the area of extreme. The range of emotion (just like all things in life) should remain in moderation.

Deficient emotional responses negate proper action because it doesn't spur you to act, excess pushes you over the limit into extreme reactions, while moderation keeps things in balance. Emotional turmoil improperly dealt with can cause deficiency or excesses in performance.

The human being's greatest strength is his capacity to love, but if love is mismanaged, improperly applied, or incorrectly regulated it takes on a duplicitous mask and becomes a destructive force that destroys the person wearing the mask and the target of its "affection."

Miseducation coupled with emotional immaturity reinforces misinformation on how to deal with emotions and fosters childish reactions to the war raging within the man when choosing how to deal with the *force* called emotion. Emotional turmoil takes place or sets up camp in the mind but uses precise attacks from behind the wall of negative feelings and negative self-talk.

- What does turmoil look like on the battlefield of your emotion, (i.e. how does your emotion fluctuate?) and what negative forms of expression did you use against your woman or women in general?

Emotional Driver

How does an Emotionally Immature mind that's struggling with how to deal with Emotional Turmoil navigate his thought maps through fear, pain, shame, frustration, and guilt? Emotions are powerful and can be the driving force that compels behavior that is harmful to self and to others.

When someone is triggered by some external stimulus (betrayal, loss, humiliation, etc.) it becomes the vehicle that drives the internal motivation to seek some form of revenge against the one who caused the pain. An emotional driver has the ability to shut down rational thinking and also can hinder the correct responses in any given moment.

Highly intelligent and powerful men have been crippled (in the area of their thinking) because when their emotion crossed over into the area of excess and took the form of an emotional driver, negative self-talk took over and unhealthy forms of expression became the vehicle to execute its attacks, i.e. hitting, manipulation, verbal abuse, being controlling, cheating, murder). The acts can be purposely mean, cruel, and instantaneous in nature, or develop over time.

Emotional intelligence that men can use when they've been educated and trained on how to deal with internal and external triggers becomes null and void when an emotional driver takes ahold of them. It's almost as if the man is experiencing a system overload, and the emotional intelligence that is necessary to handle the situation (in a morally correct way) becomes mentally blocked, and the anti-social mindset kicks in taking on the form of bitterness, bullying, aggression, hostility, cynicism, lack of empathy, lack of compassion, and hatred.

- Has something /someone compelled you to become reckless, impulsive, evil, vindictive, violent, or abusive? If so, what underlying/internal personality traits made it possible for this external event to push you to the point of losing control?

EMOTIONAL BLACKMAIL

Blackmail has its roots in coercion. To place upon a person a burden to follow what they had not initially wanted to do, based upon what *you* want them to do. To extort and coerce in the realm of a relationship there must be a desire for one person to gain an advantage over his/her partner.

Blackmail is always an unwanted position by the person being blackmailed. Always! Otherwise, there would be no need to deceptively *force* the other person to submit or comply with something they would do freely.

The emotional blackmail used can happen in the form of threats of suicide, violence, or to leave her; to commit suicide, to report her to some authority that can have an adverse effect upon her person, manipulating her to do illegal things, put-downs that tear at her self-worth and self-esteem cornering her mentally, mind games that handcuff her to unwanted positions (usually for the purpose of isolation), and using various manipulation tactics that weaponize emotions to the detriment of the woman being blackmailed.

Emotional blackmail can happen in *any* relationship, but it is much more effective when it is in the realm of a romantic relationship because the emotion shared is much more intimate in nature, and "love" can be a much more persuasive tool when seeking to coerce someone to obey/submit to a command. The deception of emotional blackmail makes it appear on the surface that everything is being done for the best interest of the woman, but in all actuality, it is the tool of the deceiver to gain power and control.

The advantage. Emotional blackmail is mental, but the end result is always manifested physically because the blackmail leads the one being blackmailed to act.

Always Harmful.

Always Unwanted.

Always Negative.

Always A Tool for The Emotionally Immature

Male Seeking Power and Control.

CHAPTER TWO

The Male Chauvinist-Arrogance and Superiority

Male Chauvinist - a man with a chauvinistic belief in the inferiority of women.

Chauvinist - a person convinced of the superiority of their own gender or kind.

Chauvinism - activity indicative of a belief in the superiority of men over women.

The belief in the position of a man's superiority over women automatically places them in a position of inferiority or at the least less than. This level of arrogance dehumanizes, devalues, and diminishes a woman's worth. When men view women through this lens it makes it easy to abuse, humiliate, manipulate, and/or degrade women. Superiority gives men a sense of entitlement and a feeling of control over the inferior
"woman" viewing her status more like a little girl or daughter, robbing her of autonomy, liberty, equality, and her basic human rights. The male chauvinist

usually has an inflated ego and a false sense of pride. Ego is defined as:

Ego: having an exaggerated sense of self-importance; an inflated feeling of pride in your superiority to others.

Egocentric: a self-centered person with little regard for others.

The ego plays an influential role in how the chauvinist process information about himself, "his" woman, and women in general. The ego has a desire to be fed and catered to, not just by others, but mainly by his most intimate partner (his woman). When these needs are not met there is a mechanism that kicks in (by default) that defends the state of the ego and its needs. The chauvinist stands on his pedestal of superiority and operating from this egotistical platform has little or no regard for "his" woman (his possession) interest. It's all about him. Arrogant. Superior. Self-centered. Controlling. Entitled.

Traditions passed downplay a major role in how the belief system is wired into young boys who become grown, male chauvinist. When boys witness certain behaviors by his first role model (his father), the males in his immediate environment (uncles, older boys, adult males on his street,) and through movies, music, and media it starts him on the road to being a chauvinist with an inflated ego and a sense of superiority over women. Thoughts inculcated like…

"Women wash the dishes, fold clothes, vacuum the floor, and make a man's food."

"Quit acting like a little B*$@h."

"Men don't cry that's for females."

"Quit working with feelings like a little girl."

"Men bring home the bacon so a woman can cook it."

or

"God made Eve for Adam," instill into the minds of young boys a belief system that says women are less than, women are weak, women do what I tell them to do (under my control), women are my possession, and/or women were made by God to have my babies and to meet my needs.

A slew of thoughts become reinforced when young boys see that inequality has a pay-value. Not necessarily a monetary pay value, but a physical pay value. One that feeds the ego and inflates a man's sense of pride and self-importance. Raising his high self-esteem at the expense of "his" woman. Chauvinism is a character defect that most men don't recognize.

A character defect is something that affects the person or someone else in a negative way. When a person has a particular mode of doing something and as a result, it affects self and others in a negative way that behavior should be analyzed, recognized, and identified as a character defect, and the person should strive to eradicate it based upon the negative impact it continuously has on self and others.

The ego in its excess refuses to accept and recognize the need for change. It (the ego) is operating from two debilitating mental roadblocks: ***Arrogance and Conceit***. The ego is fueled by arrogance and based upon a (subconscious) position of superiority in thought, opinion, word, and deed, the end result is always: ***My way trumps all others*** with no room for others' point of view, but especially "his" woman.

Rigid in his position of superiority over women the chauvinist repeats a cycle of abuse, degradation, dehumanization, and debasement of every woman he encounters. Whether openly or latently hostile when met with resistance the chauvinist repetitively denies women their liberty and rights as equal human beings.

Chauvinists usurp women's rights based upon the original view of "she is ***my*** possession" and as a result of this frame of reference dehumanize her, take away her choice, objectify her, degrade, belittle, and use her as I see fit. Always out to dominate her mind, body, and soul for my benefit. Why? Because she is my woman possession.

CHAPTER THREE

Trauma and Misogyny
(The 1st and 2nd self)

Trauma: a disordered psychic behavioral state resulting from mental or emotional stress or physical injury.

Traumatic: psychologically painful.

Trauma: an emotional wound or shock often having long-lasting effects.

Self: the entire person of an individual; an individual's temporary behavior or character.

First: the original occurrence or item of its kind; before another in time.

Second: **Alternate; Other;** slightly flawed and does not meet the manufacturer's standard for firsts.

Psychologically things can seem to be normal, but we don't always recognize how trauma plays a major role in how we process information and ultimately how we deal with people on a daily basis. Our in-real-time behavior. Trauma can create a negative, pessimistic, and mistrustful disposition towards a life circumstance and the people we interact with on a daily basis. Before a person experiences trauma, they are living as their original self (the 1st self). The self that is unblemished and unsullied by the world.

There's a freedom that comes with living as your 1st self. Our innate character is given to the world without precautions. Our trust level is at its apex. Our understanding extends far and wide. Kindness is a face that we give the world freely. Then life happens. Trust, kindness, and understanding become vulnerabilities and perceived weakness.

Different painful life experiences little by little begin to tarnish who we are internally. The pain of these experiences become our gage/template from which we make our choices. Pain, fear, shame, and guilt create a pattern of thinking that's geared toward defense. Defense against real or perceived threats that attack the person's 1st self (the vulnerable self).

The funny thing about a defense mechanism (in our thinking) is that it has the ability to keep others from getting in, but it also can be a system that keeps us (mentally) stagnated and arrested in our development. So instead of learning how to properly process pain, fear, shame, or guilt, we function (in our thinking) from a place of pain, fear, shame, and guilt. Immature and undeveloped.

Behind a mental/emotional wall (our defense mechanisms) we remain in bondage to our own past pain and disappointments. Living in a prison of our own design we are proactive about our own destructive anti-social choices and behaviors. The 2nd self when operating from a place of duplicity creates a victim of women in every facet of her being:

1. Physically she can suffer physical violence, sleeping disorders, neglect eating, alcohol & drug use, self-mutilation.

2. Emotionally she experiences sadness insecurities, confusion, guilt, shame, fear, and anger.

3. Financially there are out-of-pocket expenses, loss of wages, insurance deductibles, and increased premiums, (if physical violence occurred).

4. Socially become withdrawn from friends, family, and normal activities, distrust of people, other fractured relationships, isolation.

5. spiritually she questions God about the emptiness her soul feels because of the "love" she experiences; also questioning whether people are inherently good or evil.

6. Psychologically a fear of always being alone, nightmares, difficulty with normal relationships, difficulty with normal sexual relationships, depression, crying outbursts, and/or an inability to feel clean.

The impact of a relationship criminal operating in his 2nd self always victimizes the woman/women in his life and it usually can be traced back to the pain caused to him when he was living in his 1st self. The trauma of a bad break-up can be the original impetus that transitions the 1st self into the 2nd self.

The emotionally immature male who can't properly process emotions and the progression that occurs goes into his primitive brain (emotional survival mode) and operates from a place that is emotionally unhealthy and physically harmful to all women henceforth. The 2nd self is internal defensive thinking that manifests external offensive behavior.

Tommy's 1st and 2nd self: I was in a relationship with a woman who I loved with all of my heart & soul. In my youthful ignorance, I told myself with 100% certainty that this relationship would never end.

Not only did the relationship end, but the young woman who I had fallen madly in love with lied to me, committed adultery, became a prostitute, had a child with another man, and then divorced me. My heart was shattered. The pain and the shame seemed unbearable, and for a very long time, I wallowed in the misery of that broken relationship.

Over time that pain and shame turned into hate and a grudge that birth resentment against women strong enough to justify retaliation. To me, *all* women were whores who would betray me and eventually leave me heartbroken and alone.

I went from loving women to hating them and automatically being distrustful of their motives. I had become a misogynist before I could even spell or define the word. I was officially in my 2nd self, and the protective (emotional) skin that I created came with two mottos: trust no b***h and having 1 b***h is too close to having no b*$@h.

I functioned in duplicity to make these mottos a reality. I convinced myself that I would never allow another woman to break my heart again and I removed that possibility by having multiple women at one time, never investing too much of my heart, and always striking first. Lie first. Cheat first. Leave, first.

With my 2nd self firmly established I functioned from a place of pre-contemplation because in my mind nothing was wrong with my behavior and it was the women who had the problem because they were all whores who *deserved* to be mistreated and used.

Every woman I met was viewed as a victim and not a potential life partner. So financially, sexually, and emotionally I sought maximum usage. I would drain all the finances I could, not caring about her financial obligations (bills, insurance, food, clothes, etc.,). In my mind my needs were primary and hers were secondary. The arrogant and superior chauvinist within me said audaciously,

"If you want to be with me, you're gonna break bread, kick-in, or kick rocks." There was no middle course, my way or no way. Sexually I objectified her body for my own sexual gratification. There was no value and worth placed on her person. *My* lust…*my* desire…*my* erection…*my* climax—That is all that mattered.

Sexually I removed love. All women became to me was flesh to be used.

Emotionally I would give of myself, but secreted internal limitations and duplicitous intentions. The charlatan at work. The emotionality that I did convey was ego-driven and fed the conceit in my superiority complex. I hated women, but I needed to be loved by them. I didn't feel whole & complete without a woman's validation. My paradox was that I needed to be needed by someone my heart claimed to hate. My worth and value as a man rested in a woman's approval of me and desire for me.

I needed to be needed. I invested some emotion because it felt good to have it reciprocated, but never all (2nd self "trust no b*$@h") because I always feared being hurt. I functioned in dysfunction (my pre-contemplative 2nd self) and created victims in every relationship I entered into and exited without a conscience.

Why? Because "having one b*$@h is too close to having no b*$@h "

CHAPTER FOUR

Chameleon

Chameleon: Changeable, inconstant; a fickle person.

Changeable: subject to change; able or apt to vary; fickle.

Inconstant: likely to change frequently often without apparent or cogent reason.

Fickle: marked by erratic, unstable changes in affection, attachments, interest, loyalty, etc. unreliable or treacherous.

Chameleon's hide in plain sight in a relationship, and adapts to the moods and habits of a woman, not for the purpose of growth and development, but to survive in a stagnant state, manipulate outcomes, and/or conceal true intentions, keeping pain, inequality, and domestic violence on a perpetual cycle.

The chameleon's colors serve as camouflage, helping it blend in with its surroundings.

Acute fears such as abandonment, betrayal, inadequacies, etc. go unresolved and the build-up only reinforces the deception and fickle nature of the chameleon.

Feelings overtime left unresolved develop resentment and usually grudges that play themselves out in specific ways such as passive-aggressive verbal and/or physical abuse, retaliation in the form of deception (cheating & lying), and emotional blackmail that leaves a woman feeling handcuffed to an unwanted position.

Keeping up a false appearance can be for the sake of a perceived "security" need and relationship survival, but because the appearance is not authentic and has its roots in the deception of misleading women visually it causes the woman to be confused or to process information wrong about the true intentions of her man, which violates the trust and sow's dissension within the relationship.

Characteristics learned in childhood by parents/caregivers, through media outlets, (such as television, movies, music, etc.), at school, or in the immediate environment play a big role. It determines how much men become abusers, domestically violent, and the chameleon's in their environments.

Especially in intimate partner relationships because this is the most influential relationship that men have, and if a boy was taught chauvinism, male privilege, bravado, etc., then arrogance, entitlement, and power & control become the impetus behind decision making. If all else fails the chameleon blends into lie-and-wait for the opportunity to regain control, thus utilizing manipulation, deception, and premeditation to achieve an outcome favorable to the man seeking control.

*Chameleons feign the color of kindness, compassion, and love while beneath their exterior is the color of contempt, selfishness, and duplicity.

Holding all women in contempt for the pain of a failed marriage and a perceived betrayal I told myself that no woman would ever break my heart again. I sought to *practice* deception & duality and how to manipulate women for monetary gain and physical gratification.

Blending into her emotion I adapted to her moods, likes, and dislikes; I embellished my level of attraction, the depth of my emotion, and the loyalty of my commitment. feigning authenticity, desire, and love, all the while duplicitous in my intention, and selfishly concealing my life's motto…

"I, I, I," (me, myself & I) and,

"Having one b*$@h is too close to having no b*$@h," and,

"Trust no b*$@h."

I lied, blended in, and became a parasite. I was willing to live off the lifeblood of women, but also retaliate from within her emotions and erode her self-worth, utilizing two faces to practice deception and feign love.

Adaptation vs. Development.

Movement vs. Progress.

Intelligent, persuasive, charismatic, but duplicitous, deceptive, and immoral.

A RELATIONSHIP CRIMINAL

Where did I first learn to blend in for the purposes of protecting myself from harsh elements or to achieve some sort of personal gratification?

MANIPULATION is defined as: to control or play upon by artful, unfair, or insidious means esp. to one's own advantage. Manipulators take every opportunity to gain an advantage, but mainly at the expense of other people.

At one point in my life, my only objective was to use women. A wounded immature little boy, I allowed my thoughts to be centered on how to manipulate, abuse, degrade, and take from women. Every mental and physical tactic I could employ would be used to manipulate my way into a woman's emotions. If sex and lust were her weakness, I flaunted my physical features to lure her and exploit that weakness to my advantage. If intelligence, smooth-talking, and pretty words stimulated her mind I said whatever necessary to pry my way into her emotion.

Getting into a woman's emotions was always the primary objective. I learned early on that emotions could be exploited, weaponized, and used to my benefit and to her detriment. So, in *real time* what does that look like?

I met a woman named "Lacey." As we talked, I noticed the lust in her gaze and the way she lingered too long looking at my chest and arms. On my end, the attraction was *not* there, but I saw an opening and could *use* her own emotion (lust) against her. Seeking whatever benefits she had to offer, I feigned an equal attraction.

My intentions were to deceive her which would lead to an opening for communication I could use. That information would further my duplicity as a strategy to gain an advantage, get my needs met, and eventually discard her when she was no longer of use to me.

Manipulation became my most effective tool and my go-to tactic to achieve whatever outcome I desired using analytics, calculations, premeditation, clever schemes, and a host of other insidious & unfair stratagems to outwit unsuspecting women. Always a ruse. Always a trick. Always a charlatan. If manipulation has its roots in being unfair to another human being what underlying personality traits allowed me to hurt others intentionally despite the negative consequences?

DECEPTION is defined as: the act of deceiving; misleading; Trick; to cause to accept as true or valid what is false or invalid; to give a false impression.

Deception for me took on many faces. My goal was to mislead women and I used multiple tactics to achieve the most favorable outcome. It always began with a lie and the intent was to leave women helpless and defenseless against whatever ploy I used to achieve my outcome. Deception is a two-edged sword that cuts the victim and the person wielding the sword as well. I was deceiving women, but I was unaware that the first person who I was deceiving was myself.

The more that I told lies to women (and to myself) the more my reality became a place of delusion. Not being able to decipher my own lies, I lived in a dichotomy that ingrained itself into my character, until I had a duality that became the natural way that I processed information.; an impostor, driven by conscious and subconscious contradiction. Taking the option to lay down in a bed of lies and false realities, rather than to stand on a foundation of truth. Telling lies even in those times when the truth was good enough. Deception became my truth. An oxymoron by definition, and extremely compound ignorance.

How have I allowed the deception of my past to contribute to the deception in my present?

Men who carry shame and/or contempt for the normal feelings they had as little boys about sexuality, sensitivities, or physical postures that don't correlate with real "manhood" act out these hurt feelings in unhealthy ways in their relationship i.e. sexual violence, verbal/emotional/psychological abuse, or overt masculinity meant to exert dominance over his woman. Men suffering from different unresolved traumas think their behavior is normal but, in all actuality, they are just acting out a mechanism learned in childhood that aided in the protection of their own unmanaged and unresolved feelings.

The human spirit is fragile in its adolescence, but tradition passes down misinformation that miseducates young boys on the process it takes to become young men, and thus stunts their emotional growth, fertilizing the potential abuser within with aggression, force, and multiple forms of violence, leaving feelings unmanaged and unresolved. A little boy hiding in a man's body. A chameleon in training.

These behaviors serve a purpose that isn't immediately recognizable but feeds the ego and protect the man from further harm/pain. And because the little boy within the man never learned how to deal with pain correctly, he acts from his primitive brain.

He does what he feels is necessary, and what is normal, and if that does not work, he becomes compliant to blend in to appear as if these feelings aren't lying dormant (compliant with a deceptive purpose).

Because time reveals all things, the old adage appears, "hurt people hurt people." The abuse continues, just in another form and executed in a different way. The Chameleon at work.

There are three (3) different things that little boys do in childhood that is ultimately carried over into adulthood when incorrectly taught how to handle difficulty, pain, disappointment, rejection, or confrontation. They either make an attempt to control, comply or avoid the situation altogether.

- CONTROL - use "advice" to convince others to bend to their will use flamboyant and superficial charm to win over others; (CHARLATAN) bravado and sexual prowess become weaponized when communication fails, blame & shame to exploit emotionality of the situation, utilize deception or any means necessary (including violence) to shift the power in his balance.

- COMPLIANCE - fears expressing how they feel in order to satisfy others, wants love but will be satisfied with sex or contrite relationships, to have needs met relinquishes self to please others or to get along, acquiesces but holds on to latent resentment and grudges that manifest later, hyper-vigilant to do for others while neglecting self-care that makes him better.

- AVOIDANCE - evasive communication allows real issues to remain unaddressed, suppress how they feel in order to evade vulnerability, avoids true intimacy in order to maintain a distance that keeps them feeling "safe" wants close relationships but when things get too close becomes extremely fearful and sabotages the relationship with blatant negative behavior.

Not dealing with so many unresolved feelings and emotions as a child I learned in my environment that "men don't cry," "emotions are for females," "never show weakness," and to "man up!" At all costs. When I reached my adulthood, I was a skilled chameleon who did not deal with how I was feeling. I adapted to my environment, even if it meant exercising duplicity, duality, and deception to gain an advantage, not feel weak, and to be in a position of control.

QUESTIONS TO THINK ABOUT

Why has power and control held such importance in your life, and once you gained it (power and control) what emotional need did you satisfy as a result of gaining it?

Can you think of a time in the past (or present) that control, compliance, or avoidance became your method of handling a problem in your relationship? If so why?

CHAPTER FIVE

Cheating & Lying – The Charlatans Duality

Cheat: a deception for profit to yourself.

Cheating: engaging in deceitful behavior.

Lying: the deliberate act of deviating from the truth.

Lie: pretend with the intent to deceive.

Charlatan: a flamboyant deceiver; FRAUD; one who attracts with tricks & jokes

Cheating and lying is a morally reprehensible act that is despicable based upon its intent and eventual outcome. CHEATING AND LYING ALWAYS HURTS OUR PARTNER. Cheating and lying go hand-in- hand. The behaviors are subtle and cumulatively harmful and always designed to deceive. When a man cheats in a relationship it can be traced to one of two things, or both: 1) unchecked lust/sexual desire for another woman outside the relationship or 2) dissatisfaction with the quality of the relationship.

The mentality of the charlatan is different because he *enters* the relationship with the intent to deceive and deliberately dupe/trick the woman he's with. From the relationship's inception, the woman is being used, abused, and victimized. The trust in which a relationship is built upon is violated, and the woman is unknowingly entrapped by lies as she falls for the charlatan's con.

Whether cheating and lying happen, as a result of unchecked lust, discontented relationship issues, or blatant/intentional trickery, the end result is always the same: a woman left hurt and victimized.

Cheating and lying is an ugly act that has its roots in deception. The mentality of deception gives permission slips to harm another human being. It is a pattern of denial (of the effects of duplicity). The charlatan rationalizes *why* his behavior is acceptable.

To examine the roots of men's deceptive behavior we must trace it to its origin. So the question to be considered is: Who is the first person who taught you the act of deception?

To bring it forward the question is: How would *you* feel if *you* were cheated on, lied to, and victimized by someone you trusted?

When a charlatan pretends to entertain one set of intentions while acting under the influence of another it speaks to the duality that exists in his character. In order to function in the character of a charlatan (a flamboyant deceiver), there must exist an internal dichotomy that drives/fuels this unhealthy & immoral behavior. Unhealthy because it either harms self or others. Immoral because of its dishonesty and refusal to adhere to ethical principles of virtue and sexual morality.

The charlatan is a bonafide imposter. Women are duped by his charm and "helpful" nature which in all actuality is a covert strategic manipulation. Stratagems are carefully crafted to camouflage true intention. Everything becomes weaponized (i.e. physical features and forms of expression, sex, charm, gentlemanly assistance, advice, time, gifts, etc.) in the arsenal of the charlatan, even "love."

In the charlatan's mind "my needs will be met by any means necessary." Until he is unmasked and exposed the elaborate deception knows no end. The charlatan's behavior becomes so deeply ingrained in his character/personality until eventually his conscience is silenced and severed from its innate nature to protect, nurture, love, honor, and protect his mate.

If any contemplation occurs regarding the fraudulent nature of his behavior the thought is squelched by an unscrupulous conscience bent on its own desires. Love when it is noble, brings upon the highest forms of heavenly goodness, but when it is debased leads to the lowest sins and the worst relationship crimes. Hence the charlatan. The relationship criminal.

CHAPTER SIX

The Cycle of Emotional Intelligence

The road to emotional maturity begins with an understanding of the power of four elements: *Intellect, Free Will, Spirituality, and Emotions,* and how they correlate with one another to bring upon in-real-time behaviors. The man who learns how to bring these four powerful elements of the human being into balance officially transitions into the realm of emotional maturity.

How do we connect mind, choice, faith, and feeling in our real-life experiences? First, let's look at these elements individually and then in conjunction with one another working for the greater good of the individual.

- **Intellect**:

The power of the intellect in its excess becomes a defense mechanism that uses reasoning to block out emotional stress. The intellect will subconsciously use its memory (past experiences) to create safe thought patterns that will rationalize any situation to justify an extreme, immoral, or irrational choice. The intellect will place the greatest importance on itself, negating the importance of context, timing, ambiance, and other pertinent facts that help the mind formulate a proper response.

When the intellect is functioning from memory by default all it recognizes is the pain of a past situation and its main resolve is to avoid the pain it once experienced. Past pain and disappointment if improperly processed stunts a boy's growth & development (emotionally) and accelerates his intellect on how to avoid future situation s that resemble the pain he once experienced. The brain (mind) is a masterful tool and when it's in its extreme/excess, negating or divorcing emotion, it artfully weaves together machinations bent on preservation of self.

The intellect standing alone can clearly articulate its ideas and ideals, but when asked to articulate itself emotionally it becomes reticent or without emotional depth. The intellect if left standing alone (i.e. negating all other pertinent & relevant factors such as context, ambiance, etc.) ceases to be a tool of power and paradoxically becomes a tool of unintelligence based upon the emotionless choices it makes.

- **Free Will:**

When Free Will functions alone it focuses on its own desires. The lusts of the heart can have a gravitational attraction strong enough to sway the strongest of men to sin. Be it food, gambling, intoxicants, sex, power, or greed, when the free will of man is in its excess left unrestrained & unchecked it can/will indulge itself in the sinfulness of its nature and become a "free willing" slave to its own vices. Coarsely gluttonous and greedy for its selfish pleasures. It's been said that a strong man is not one who can take control of an entire nation, but one who can take control of himself. Why? Because the desires of man's heart can be an uncontrollable force within. himself, and when in collaboration with his free will it usually leads to compulsion.

The free will of man when left standing alone can become a destructive force laced with sinful desire. The free will when in its excess and in the grips of its vices operates from a pleasure principle that violates moral law. Free will has the ability to debase man to his animalistic/fleshly form, and his appetites and passions become his god and the impetus behind his daily choices.

The mind abandons its superior thought capabilities which rises man to vicegerent of the earth, and when he relinquishes that control, he lowers himself to his instinctual nature that craves food, sex, and power. His base needs. Driven by the carnal appetites that divorce rational thought, man in his animalistic free will does not adhere to ethical or moral principles, and where intellect does seep in it becomes subjective rationalizations that are geared toward meeting the needs of the (ID) pleasure principle.

Free will without a checking mechanism that establishes order and distinguishes needs v. wants, can become a destructive emotional & instinctual force severed from discretion. Free will when working in accordance with other necessary elements is a natural condition of the human psyche, but when working in concert (only) with its own base nature becomes a detriment to the physical or moral well-being of the person.

- **Emotions**:

  Emotional responses are determined or actuated by feeling rather than logic or reason. When emotions are aroused, and triggered impulsivity can be an impelling and unpredictable force. Things are done on a whim rather than by logic or necessity. Emotions bring upon decisions in haste and in many instances without taking or considering necessary cautions.

A person who usually acts in emotion alone has that trait of acting suddenly and capriciously on impulse without proper reflection. All choices have pros & cons, risk v. reward, and positive/negative consequences. When emotions become the primary mode for decision-making feelings are facts and deified as truth above any logical or factual argument. Feelings are subjective, whimsical, and if functioning alone in its extreme dangerously unstable. Emotion (feeling) can be very fickle.

The person functioning from emotion alone becomes a wild card that can change the trajectory of any given situation or circumstance based upon a feeling, not logic or reason. What's difficult for the overly emotional being is differentiating (or learning to distinguish) between experiencing a raw emotion and the choice made on how to express it.

Emotions are a force that can control a being and bring upon a very unhealthy imbalance. Finality in choice comes as a result of what is felt rather than calculations made based upon all pertinent and relevant factors. How many times have you seen a highly intelligent person spiral out of control or make a terrible choice? The reason is that they were in the grips of raw emotion (i.e. fear, pain, shame, anger, lust, or greed) and it short-circuited their ability to make a wise choice based upon their intellect.

The force of an uncontrolled emotion can be like a tidal wave that floods every fiber in the human psyche, and the primitive instinctual brain (The ID) focuses on what feels good and flee from what feels painful. The prevailing theme becomes "if it feels right then it must be right" because the overly emotional person's emotions (feelings) are facts.

The overly emotional being can also be in a state of pre-contemplation and see nothing wrong with their behavior (because feelings are facts) or lean heavily on denial patterns that justify, minimize, or rationalize why the emotional choice superseded a rational choice. An overly emotional being runs hot and cold and demonstrates a pattern of instability in their character making them very difficult to be around.

The up & down roller coaster personality has extreme highs and extreme lows that become social repellants arousing aversion or disgust from those around them. This type of individual when they're on a high everything's fantastic, but when they're on a low watch out. They exhibit (either verbally or non-verbally) a level of anger sadness or depression that infects or taints anyone in their vicinity.

The problem with an individual who deifies emotion is that emotions need an intellectual component- and vice versa - because it brings balance and without this connection active in our decision making it can be chaotic and depending on the circumstance disastrous.

- **Spirituality**:

Spirituality when standing on its own can create a rigid inflexibility that places supreme importance on a matter that locks an individual into one fixed position. When spiritual/religious matters are viewed as the highest authority (in all matters) it has the ability to overlook the human element of life interactions.

There was once a man considered to be the most pious man in the land, and he would spend many hours throughout the day in prayer and supplication. He had two beautiful grandsons that loved him dearly and there would be times when he was in prayer and supplication that his grandsons would begin to crawl all over him, pull at his clothes, and disturb his spiritual/religious obligations. They wanted to spend time with him.

Instead of scolding his grandsons or pushing them off to the side he shortened his spiritual time and tended to their needs. He understood that if he did turn them away, admonish or scold them, it would have a negative impact upon 1) how they would grow up to view prayer & supplication 2) their desire for a relationship with their grandfather 3) their emotional health, and 4) their future relationship with God. He understood his duties and obligations to his Lord, but he also understood his duties and obligations as a grandfather and had the foresight to see how being in one case would have a negative impact on the other. He effectively balanced the two.

The mentality of the spiritually rigid can only view life through a narrow-minded lens. Spirituality is very important, but not all-important. Spirituality gives us a moral compass and when we follow a specific religion there is a Holy Book that has rules & laws that we must follow. For example, the Bible teaches that we should do charity and give to others in need, but should we give our neighbors everything we have leaving our own shelves bare. A strictly religious/spiritual position is a narrow-mindedness that doesn’t' consider all pertinent factors. Because of the moral component of spiritual & religious decision making it leads one to believe that it is the best choice while negating the negative impact it could be having in other ways.

An overly spiritual person can also live in one of two extremes 1) In a lackadaisical way where the thought patterns say "I'm just gonna' have faith and wait on the Lord to provide my needs" and 2) I'm (Christian, Muslim, or Jewish) therefore I'm better than you.

The holier-than-thou mentality exhibits arrogance and conceit that attaches excessive pride. Also, it removes the pious humility and modesty that spiritual & religious matters are supposed to instill within the person. Spirituality when standing on its own can be a rigid way of living. Spirituality thus can become a form of self-righteousness.

If the view of the other person does not jibe with what their spiritual/religious beliefs are they are written off as non-believers. Spiritual teachings become their highest source of guidance. All other forms of education are written off and a spiritual wall is placed between the person and the information being transmitted.

CHAPTER SEVEN

Mind, Will, Feeling, and Faith in Balance

The balance between Thinking, Choosing, Faith, and Feeling is not always an easy thing to do. Especially when one element is out of balance and in its excess. The proper use of the mind, free will, faith, and emotion bring equilibrium and holistic balance. The equality of distribution brings stability that is beneficial to the overall functioning of man in real-time.

Decisions made in balance that weigh all pertinent factors are usually rational and sound. For the emotionally mature man, there must be a combination of these four elements working together with an equal amount of consideration applied to each. When these elements are in congruence it brings upon a stable character and usually a positive personality.

The balance of these four elements acts as an adhesive to the personality and character. It becomes the binding agent of a stable being who makes wise/sound decisions. When any of these four elements are out of balance the lens from which a person views the world becomes skewed, completely blocked, or at the least incomplete.

Just like cement if one element of its mixture is off it weakens the finished product. Too much of this, too little of that, or if it doesn't set long enough renders the *process* incomplete and when the pressure of a life situation happens the cement cracks under pressure, rendering it defective (a *Character* defect).

To be out of balance emotionally is to be living in an unhealthy extreme that trusts gut feeling over all other senses. The emotionally unhealthy person is one who utilizes every available lens when making choices. Covering every angle allows for widescreen thinking that sees everything in the picture.

The view that sees intellectually (the facts), spiritually (the moral compass), emotionally (the compassion of the heart), and with free will (the power of choice). This view is holistic and brings upon a better chance for decisions to be sound and for outcomes to be healthy and in a just balance.

Everything in life has a natural order. The trees, plants, gravity, and the ocean all function under a natural order. It's the will of our Creator. When things are out of balance it has an immediate negative ripple effect or overtime. Either way, the impact is negative and harmful.

The inner working of the human being is no different. The Self is a community made up of emotion, memory, intellect, free will, spirituality, imagination, etc. and the moment we begin to live without balancing our inner being our personality & character lack balance, and it creates an instability in the natural order of our human condition.

About the Author

Tommy Eugene Lewis, III was born in South Central, Los Angeles, California in 1977 to parents Tommy Eugene Lewis, Jr. and Wanda Jean Hurndon. As a youth, he attended both public and private schools. After a string of bad choices, he found himself incarcerated at the age of 18, and at 20 years old in prison where his baneful behavior was only exacerbated, leaving behind a slew of victims.

Manipulation became ingrained in his character and his go-to weapon. The ripple effect of his intellect in excess had a tremendously negative impact on countless innocent victims. Mr. Lewis contemplated change in 2011 after getting a female staff member arrested and fired for bringing in drugs and cell phones. His turning point ultimately came in 2014 when the two people he loved most, Nancy Kayla Nunez and Breanna Faith Tucker, found themselves on his victim's list, while he sat in Administrative Segregation thinking how his manipulatory lifestyle made him his own victim, placing himself on that victim list.

Because his manipulation had an adverse effect upon people he loved and upon his own heart, the paradigm from which he viewed manipulation was forever changed. As a result, it caused him to look at all the people he has hurt, and the lifetime negative impact and magnitude on other's lives. Through education, self-reflection, and the application of spiritual principles, this short work was compiled in an attempt to shine the light on the Chameleon Hiding In Plain Sight, with the hopes of staving off the Cycle of Abuse and Domestic Violence that the manipulation of women produces.

Other books by Authors Inside

The Molding of Him

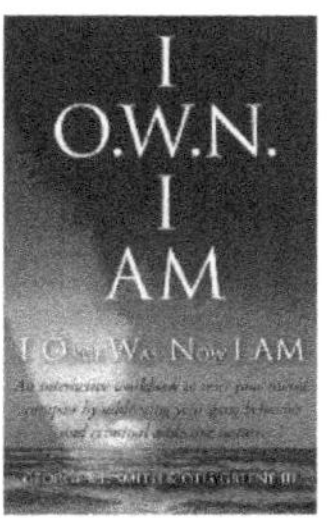

I O.W.N. I AM (I Once Was Now I Am)

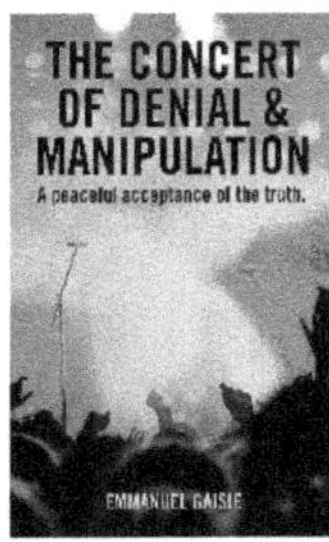

The Concert of Denial & Manipulation

Words I Never Got Spoken (how I remember juvenile hall)

Authors Inside is a 501(c)(3) nonprofit organization committed to publishing all book genres provided it advances our mission statement of, ***Making sustainable change through narrative writing, with the purpose of reducing and preventing juvenile crimes, promoting and maintaining safe communities, and improving the welfare of youth and families.***

Submissions should include a one-page summary of your manuscript mailed to PO Box 293, Oceano, CA 93475. An approval committee will review all submissions and respond within 4-6 weeks with a request for the full manuscript if accepted. Authors Inside's goal is to publish 12 books annually, dependent on funding.

Web: http://authorsinside.org

Email: info@authorsinside.org

www.ingramcontent.com/pod-product-compliance
Lightning Source LLC
LaVergne TN
LVHW010107110826
845155LV00028B/532

* 9 7 8 1 9 5 4 7 3 6 0 4 7 *